HONDURAS 2016 HUMAN RIGHTS REPORT

EXECUTIVE SUMMARY

Honduras is a constitutional, multiparty republic. The country held national and local elections in November 2013. Voters elected Juan Orlando Hernandez of the National Party as president for a four-year term that began in January 2014. International observers generally recognized the elections as transparent, credible, and reflecting the will of the electorate. The National Congress elected a new 15-member Supreme Court for a seven-year term in February.

Civilian authorities at times did not maintain effective control over the security forces.

Pervasive societal violence persisted, although the state made efforts to reduce it. The March murder of environmental and indigenous rights activist Berta Caceres underscored state institutions' lack of effective measures to protect activists. Violence and land-rights disputes involving indigenous people, agricultural workers, landowners, the extractive industry, and development projects continued in rural areas, including the Bajo Aguan region. Organized criminal elements, including local and transnational gangs and narcotics traffickers, were significant perpetrators of violent crimes and committed acts of murder, extortion, kidnapping, torture, human trafficking, and intimidation of journalists, women, and human rights defenders.

Other serious human rights problems were widespread impunity due to corruption and institutional weaknesses in the investigative, prosecutorial, and judicial systems, and excessive use of force and criminal actions by members of the security forces. Additional, human rights problems included harsh and at times life-threatening prison conditions; lengthy pretrial detention and failure to provide due process of law; threats and violence by criminals directed against human rights defenders, judicial authorities, lawyers, the business community, journalists, bloggers, and members of vulnerable populations; violence against and harassment of women; child abuse; trafficking in persons, including child prostitution; human smuggling, including of unaccompanied children; failure to conduct free and informed consultations with indigenous communities prior to the authorization of development projects; discrimination against indigenous and Afro-descendent communities; violence against and harassment of lesbian, gay, bisexual, transgender, and intersex (LGBTI) persons; ineffective enforcement of labor laws; and child labor.

The government took steps to prosecute and punish officials who committed abuses, including arresting and prosecuting members of congress, judges, prosecutors, police officers, mayors, and other local authorities. Civilian authorities arrested and investigated members of the security forces alleged to have committed human rights abuses. Some prosecutions of military and police officials charged with human rights violations moved too slowly or failed to convict the responsible parties.

Section 1. Respect for the Integrity of the Person, Including Freedom from:

a. Arbitrary Deprivation of Life and other Unlawful or Politically Motivated Killings

There were multiple reports that the government or its agents committed arbitrary or unlawful killings.

Civilian authorities investigated and arrested members of the security forces accused of human rights abuses. Impunity, however, remained a serious problem, with delays in some prosecutions and sources alleging corruption in judicial proceedings.

On March 3, environmental and indigenous activist, Berta Caceres, was killed in her home in Intibuca Department (see also section 6, Indigenous People). In early May the Public Ministry arrested five individuals implicated in her killing, including an active duty Honduran Special Forces officer and a manager at a hydroelectric project that Caceres had actively opposed. Law enforcement authorities arrested a sixth suspect in September. As of November a judge had remanded all six to custody pending trial, and their defense lawyer had submitted a request for dismissal of the charges, which was still pending. The Public Ministry continued its investigation into whether others were involved in planning the crime. The Honduran Armed Forces dishonorably discharged the Special Forces officer implicated in Caceres' death.

Also in March local and international media reported that corrupt senior police officials working for drug traffickers were responsible for the killings of senior antinarcotics officials Julian Gonzalez in 2009 and Alfredo Landaverde in 2011, and the murder of senior anti-money-laundering prosecutor Orlan Chavez in 2013. According to media reports, other senior police and Ministry of Security officials covered up the crimes or failed to take action to bring those responsible to justice.

Subsequently, the government passed legislative decree 21-2016, which created the Special Commission in Charge of Purging and Restructuring the Honduran National Police (HNP), comprising the minister of security, a former president of the Supreme Court, and two prominent members of civil society, to review systematically the performance and integrity of all police officials. As of December 19, the commission had reviewed the personnel files of 3,004 officials and dismissed 1,835 officers, while allowing 256 officers to retire voluntarily, for a total of 2,091 police officers dismissed from the HNP. In February a three-judge tribunal acquitted all senior military officials previously accused of covering up the 2012 killing of 15-year-old Ebed Jassiel Yanes Caceres.

On May 19, Military Police for Public Order (PMOP) soldier, Jose Alonzo Miranda Almendarez, shot and killed Alexis Alberto Avila Ramirez when Avila and his brother fled from the PMOP squad executing arrest warrants against them in the city of Danli, El Paraiso Department. A judge ruled there was sufficient evidence to hold Miranda on a charge of abuse of authority and manslaughter pending a trial; his defense requested a dismissal of the charges, and an appeals court was reviewing the appeal as of October. Miranda's PMOP patrol was participating in a joint operation directed by the National Interinstitutional Security Force (FUSINA), but it reported to the 110th Infantry Brigade.

In August the trial of four armed forces intelligence personnel implicated in the 2014 killings of siblings Ramon Eduardo Diaz Rodriguez and Zenia Maritza Diaz Rodriguez was scheduled to begin in February 2017.

In February a judge issued a warrant for the arrest of PMOP members involved in the shooting of 11-year-old Yoslin Isaac Martinez Rivera in November 2015. As of October the individuals had not been arrested.

Authorities arrested HNP officer, Donis Joel Figueroa Reyes, for the November 2015 torture of three detainees and murder of detainee Jose Armando Gomez Sanchez. The three individuals had been detained for public intoxication but allegedly attempted to escape detention, after which they were handcuffed to the ceiling in the police station and beaten by Figueroa, resulting in Gomez's death. Figueroa was originally detained in November 2015 but had escaped from custody.

There continued to be reports of violence related to land conflicts and criminal activity in the Bajo Aguan region, but the overall level of violence in the area was far below its 2012 peak. On October 18, Jose Angel Flores, president of the Unified Farm Workers Movement of the Aguan (MUCA) and his colleague Silmer

Dionicio George, were killed after leaving a meeting of MUCA leaders. On November 21, the Public Ministry announced arrest warrants for two individuals--Osvin Nahun Caballero and Wilmer Giovanni Fuentes--believed to be involved in the October 18 attack; the ministry stated that the murders appeared to be related to the continuing land conflict. No members of the security forces or private security guards were reported to have been responsible for deaths related to the land conflict. One private security guard of an agricultural company, however, was reportedly killed due to land conflict, and agricultural workers reported at least one other violent encounter between private security guards and agricultural workers as of August.

Organized criminal elements, including narcotics traffickers and local and transnational gangs such as MS-13 and the 18th Street gang, committed murders, extortion, kidnappings, human trafficking, and acts of intimidation against police, prosecutors, journalists, women, and human rights defenders. Major urban centers and drug trafficking routes experienced disproportionate rates of violence. Media reported that as of September 7,176 individuals working in the transportation sector had been killed during the year, often for failing to make extortion payments. The Violence Observatory of the National Autonomous University of Honduras (UNAH) reported that 290 workers from the transportation sector were killed in 2015, a 40 percent increase from 2014.

On May 27, the UN special rapporteur on extrajudicial, summary, or arbitrary executions recognized that the government had taken steps to reduce the homicide rate, but urged authorities to do more to protect the right to life and reduce violence. According to the UNAH Violence Observatory, there was no significant change in the overall annual homicide rate in the first six months of the year compared with 2015, which remained at approximately 60 per 100,000 after several years of steep decline. Reports linked many of these homicides to organized crime and gangs.

b. Disappearance

The HNP reported 40 kidnappings in 2015, a 48 percent decrease from 2014. As of October the HNP projected a further 65 percent decrease in kidnappings during the year. The HNP reported that in 2015 it rescued 28 victims. Nine more were freed through negotiations and partial payment. Kidnappers killed three others. As of October the HNP had rescued 16 victims. The HNP estimated that it prevented 80 million lempiras ($3.2 million) in ransom payments to criminals in 2015. Court cases took on average two years. In one case from 2014, the HNP rescued the victim within 24 hours and arrested a suspect. Further investigation led to two additional arrests. On July 21, all three were sentenced to 20 years in prison.

c. Torture and Other Cruel, Inhuman, or Degrading Treatment or Punishment

Although the constitution and law prohibit such practices, human rights nongovernmental organizations (NGOs) received complaints of abuse by members of the security forces on the streets and in detention centers. On August 10, the UN Committee Against Torture expressed concern over numerous reports of human rights violations, including torture, by members of the security forces. As of September the National Human Rights Commission (CONADEH) reported 221 complaints implicating members of the security forces or other government officials in torture or other cruel or inhuman treatment, whereas the quasi-governmental National Committee for the Prevention of Torture, Cruel, Inhuman, or Degrading Treatment (CONAPREV) reported 70 complaints against government officials for human rights violations, the majority relating to detention conditions. The Public Ministry had 49 active torture cases against members of police and military as of October.

In April agents from the Public Ministry's Technical Agency for Criminal Investigations arrested nine prison guards in Danli, El Paraiso Department, for allegedly torturing an inmate. Media reported that the alleged victim, Carlos Lenin Meza Navas, had lodged a complaint against a guard on February 6 for not permitting him to make an authorized telephone call. The guard and eight of his colleagues subsequently assaulted Navas in his cell, beating him unconscious.

There were reports that criminal gangs tortured individuals.

Prison and Detention Center Conditions

Prison conditions were harsh and sometimes life threatening because of pervasive gang-related violence and the government's failure to control criminal activity within the prisons. Prisoners suffered from overcrowding, insufficient access to food and water, violence, and abuse by prison officials.

Following a 2014 fire in the Comayagua prison that killed 361 inmates, the National Congress approved the National Prison System Act in 2015, which modified the organization of prisons and mandated the professionalization of police charged with prison administration. In February the Inter-American Commission on Human Rights (IACHR) reported that the country's prisons still suffered from many of the same problems that contributed to the 2014 Comayagua tragedy. These problems included the delegation of internal controls to prisoners themselves and a corresponding lack of responsible management by prison authorities; overcrowding and deplorable incarceration conditions; and a failure to segregate men and women fully in most prisons.

Physical Conditions: Prisoners suffered from severe overcrowding, malnutrition, lack of adequate sanitation and medical care, and, in some prisons, lack of adequate ventilation and lighting. The Ministry of Human Rights, Justice, Governance, and Decentralization reported that as of August the total prison population was 17,253 in 27 prisons, an 8 percent increase over September 2015. According to the ministry, the system had designed capacity for approximately 10,600 inmates.

The National Prison Institute (INP) reported that as of August 12, 16 inmates had died in prison, 14 from natural causes and two from suicide. Seven inmates were killed outside prison while receiving medical care or on conditional home release. In contrast, CONAPREV reported that 19 prisoners died in altercations between inmates, three committed suicide, and four died from illness.

As of August the Ministry of Human Rights, Justice, Governance, and Decentralization reported that the country's four pretrial detention centers held 75 individuals. Three of these centers were on military installations, and the other was located on the installations of the HNP's Special Operations Command (known as COBRAS). The government used pretrial detention centers to hold high-profile suspects and those in need of additional security. The military provided some support services to the three detention centers located on military bases; however, the military neither administered them nor provided guards for the facilities. Instead, the INP oversaw them, as it did other prisons.

Due to overcrowding and lack of adequate training for prison staff, prisoners were subjected to serious abuses, including rape by other inmates. Prisons lacked trained personnel to safeguard the psychological and physical wellbeing of inmates, and some prisons lacked sufficient security personnel.

Many prisoners had access to weapons and other contraband, inmates attacked other inmates with impunity, escapes were frequent, and inmates and their associates outside prison threatened prison officials and their families. These conditions contributed to an unstable, dangerous environment in the penitentiary system. Media reported multiple prison riots and violent confrontations between gang members in prisons throughout the year. Inmates killed several prison guards, including the deputy director of the San Pedro Sula prison, either inside prison facilities or by giving orders that criminal associates on the outside carried out on their behalf.

There were credible reports from human rights organizations that, in addition to subjecting prisoners to isolation and threats, prison officials used excessive force, such as beatings, to control prisoners.

The government held approximately one-half of its female prisoners at a facility for mothers with young children and pregnant women. Others were housed in separate areas of men's prisons. In the San Pedro Sula prison, for instance, approximately 70 women resided in their own wing of the prison but shared communal space with upwards of 2,900 men. Children up to the age of three could stay with their mothers in prison. Authorities often held pretrial detainees together with convicted prisoners.

Authorities did not segregate those with tuberculosis or other infectious diseases from the general prison population; there was only limited support for persons with mental illnesses or disabilities. CONAPREV reported that every prison had a functioning health clinic with at least one medical professional, except for the National Penitentiary in Francisco Morazan Department. Basic medical supplies and medicines, particularly antibiotics, were in short supply throughout the prison system. In most prisons only inmates who purchased bottled water or had water filters in their cells had access to potable water.

As of August the NGO Casa Alianza said juvenile detention staff reported there were 438 minors (394 boys and 44 girls) in five juvenile detention centers, segregated by gender. CONAPREV, however, reported that 542 boys resided in two juvenile detention centers and the COBRAS pretrial detention center as of August. According to the Directorate of Childhood and Family, 304 youths benefited from alternative sentencing outside the juvenile detention system between January 2015 and August (see section 6, Institutionalized Children).

Administration: The INP, an autonomous agency, managed the country's adult prisons. The minister of human rights, justice, governance, and decentralization, together with the minister of security, an NGO representative, and a representative of the National Municipal Association formed a committee that supervised the

INP. Public defenders and judges sought alternatives to incarceration for nonviolent offenders as a means to alleviate prison overcrowding. Flawed recordkeeping procedures meant that some inmates served more time in prison than their sentences specified.

Prisoners could submit complaints to judicial authorities without censorship and could submit requests for the investigation of inhuman conditions directly to the director of the prison in which they were incarcerated. Directors could then transfer the complaints to the INP director. Prisoners also could file complaints with the INP's Human Rights Protection Unit, the Public Ministry's Office of the Special Prosecutor for Human Rights, and the Ministry of Human Rights, Justice, Governance, and Decentralization. CONADEH also took complaints and conducted investigations. The results of investigations by NGOs and government officials were available to the public. CONAPREV reported there were three complaints of torture and mistreatment in detention centers as of September. NGOs reported that some prisoners were reluctant to file official complaints because they did not trust the authorities and there was no effective system for witness protection (also see section 1.c.).

The 2015 Law of Obligatory Labor for Prisoners stipulates that prison populations must engage in at least 400 hours of community service per individual. Officials had not implemented the law, however, with the exception of some minor farming initiatives at the Comayagua prison (also see section 7.b.).

Independent Monitoring: The government generally permitted prison visits by independent local and international human rights observers, including the International Committee of the Red Cross. Faith-based organizations such as the San Pedro Sula-based Roman Catholic Penitentiary Pastoral engaged in small-scale rehabilitation and vocational programs with willing inmates. The Ministry of Human Rights, Justice, Governance, and Decentralization made inspection visits to pretrial detention centers. The Human Rights Protection Unit of the INP made routine inspections of prison facilities and pretrial detention centers. CONAPREV made more than a dozen visits to juvenile detention facilities as of the end of August.

Improvements: In late 2015 the government launched an initiative to reduce prison overcrowding. After reviewing a list of cases recommended by prison administrators, at the end of 2015, the government released approximately 2,000 inmates who had completed their sentences or had already been in pretrial detention for longer than the maximum sentences for their alleged crimes. The government opened two new prisons, with a capacity of 2,300 prisoners.

The Ministry of Human Rights, Justice, Governance, and Decentralization reported that as of July, it had trained 1,100 prisoners in five prisons on human rights, a culture of peace, and their responsibilities under the 2015 National Prison System Act. The Human Rights Protection Unit trained an additional 600 prisoners on their human rights and national and international standards applicable to prisoners.

The INP trained 250 staff members on human rights for prisoners; nondiscrimination; the prevention of torture and other cruel, inhuman, or degrading treatment or punishment; minimum standards for treatment of prisoners; national and international standards applicable to prisoners; and the appropriate use of lethal and nonlethal force.

Antiretroviral treatment programs expanded significantly throughout the prison system, and many HIV-positive patients who were not previously receiving treatment began a course of medication. Testing programs for HIV/AIDS, tuberculosis, and diabetes improved. On April 27, the Ministry of Human Rights, Justice, Governance, and Decentralization and INP signed an agreement with the Ministry of Health to improve prison health services. As of August the government had hired 18 doctors to staff prisons. CONAPREV reported an increase in technical personnel available to assist prisoners, including public defenders, psychologists, and social workers.

d. Arbitrary Arrest or Detention

The constitution and law prohibit arbitrary arrest and detention, but human rights NGOs reported that authorities at times failed to enforce these prohibitions effectively. CONADEH reported 12 cases of arbitrary arrest as of September. The Committee of Relatives of the Disappeared in Honduras reported 23 illegal or arbitrary arrests: five by the PMOP, 13 by the HNP, and five by municipal police.

Role of the Police and Security Apparatus

The HNP maintains internal security and reports to the Secretariat of Security. The Technical Agency for Criminal Investigations at the Public Ministry (Attorney General's Office) has legal authority to investigate 21 types of crimes and make arrests. The armed forces, which report to the Secretariat of Defense, are responsible for external security but also exercise some domestic security responsibilities. The PMOP reports to military authorities but conducts operations sanctioned by civilian security officials as well as by military leaders. As of August the PMOP had approximately 3,000 personnel organized into six battalions and was present in all 18 departments. In 2015 a total of 2,400 members of the PMOP received human rights training. FUSINA coordinates the overlapping responsibilities of the HNP, PMOP, National Intelligence Directorate, Public Ministry, and national court system. FUSINA reports to the National Security and Defense Council. The president chairs the council, which includes representatives of the Supreme Court, National Congress, Public Ministry, and Secretariats of Security and Defense.

The armed forces surrendered members accused of human rights violations to civilian authorities. The armed forces sometimes dishonorably discharged such individuals, even before a criminal trial. The Public Ministry, primarily through the Office of the Special Prosecutor for Crimes against Life, is responsible for investigating cases in which a government agent is allegedly responsible for killing a civilian. Prosecutors try such cases in civilian courts. Prosecutors and judges attached to FUSINA prosecute and hear cases related to FUSINA operations. A unit within the Office of the Special Prosecutor for Crimes against Life manages some cases of homicides committed by members of the security forces and government officials. The human rights office of the joint staff of the armed forces investigated allegations of human rights abuses by members of the armed forces.

Corruption and impunity remained serious problems within the security forces. Some members of police committed crimes, including crimes linked to local and international criminal organizations.

On April 11, in response to media reports that high-ranking HNP officers had ordered the killing of senior antinarcotics and anti-money-laundering officials in 2009, 2011, and 2013, the president approved a decree creating the Special Commission in Charge of Purging and Restructuring the HNP. The minister of security heads the commission and oversees the work of three prominent members of civil society and a small group of advisors. The commission has authority to: determine the suitability of HNP officials and dismiss officers without cause, implement a mechanism to follow-up and supervise the evaluation and dismissal processes, pass the personnel records of dismissed police officers suspected of criminal activity to the Public Ministry and the Supreme Auditing Tribunal for review and possible prosecution, and report progress to the president and National Congress on a quarterly basis.

As of mid-December the commission reported that it had evaluated 3,004 HNP officers. The commission recommended that 887 of these be retained, 1,835 dismissed, 256 voluntarily retired, 15 suspended pending further review, and another 11 retained pending further evaluation; many of those dismissed were high-ranking officers. The commission referred 23 of these officers to the Public Ministry for possible criminal prosecution. At the commission's request, the attorney general formed a special unit to investigate cases that the commission referred to it. The process has led to more dismissals than the previous five efforts undertaken since 1998 combined. The commission still needed to evaluate rank-and-file members of the HNP. The commission said the personnel it recommended for retention remained subject to continued suitability evaluations.

The Human Rights Office of the Honduran Armed Forces reported that as of August, more than 4,500 service members had received human rights training. The Honduran Armed Forces and various NGOs provided the training. The Honduran Armed Forces Cadet Leadership Development course trained approximately 220 cadets on human rights in 2015-16.

Arrest Procedures and Treatment of Detainees

The law provides that police may make arrests only with a warrant, unless they make the arrest during the commission of a crime, there is strong suspicion that a person has committed a crime and might otherwise evade criminal prosecution, they catch a person in possession of evidence related to a crime, or a prosecutor has ordered the arrest. The law requires police to inform persons of the grounds for their arrest and bring detainees before a competent judicial authority within 24 hours. It stipulates that a prosecutor then has 24 additional hours to decide if there is probable cause for indictment, whereupon a judge has 24 more hours to decide whether to issue a temporary detention order. Such an order may be effective for up to six days, after which the judge must hold a pretrial hearing to examine whether there is probable cause to continue pretrial detention. The law allows persons charged with some felonies to avail themselves of bail and gives prisoners a right of prompt access to family members. The law allows the release of other suspects pending formal charges, on the condition that they periodically report to authorities. The government generally respected these provisions. Persons suspected of any of 22 felonies must remain in custody, pending the conclusion of judicial proceedings against them; however, the Constitutional Chamber of the Supreme Court ruled during the year that when a trial is delayed excessively, prisoners may be released on the condition that they continue to report periodically to authorities. The law grants prisoners the right to prompt access to a lawyer of their choice and, if indigent, to government-provided counsel, although authorities did not always abide by these requirements.

<u>Arbitrary Arrest</u>: The Public Ministry reported 35 cases of illegal detention or arbitrary arrest as of October.

<u>Pretrial Detention</u>: Judicial inefficiency, corruption, and insufficient resources delayed proceedings in the criminal justice system, and lengthy pretrial detention was a serious problem. As of August according to the UNAH's Institute for Democracy, Peace, and Security, 53 percent of the country's prison population had not been convicted. For crimes with minimum sentences of six years, the law authorizes pretrial detention of up to two years. The prosecution may request an additional six-month extension, but many detainees remained in pretrial detention much longer, including for more time than the maximum period of incarceration for their alleged crime. The law does not authorize pretrial detention for crimes with a maximum sentence of five years or less. The law mandates that authorities release detainees whose cases have not yet come to trial and whose time in pretrial detention already exceeds the maximum prison sentence for their alleged crime. Even so, many prisoners remained in custody after completing their full sentences, and sometimes even after an acquittal, because officials failed to process their releases expeditiously.

<u>Detainee's Ability to Challenge Lawfulness of Detention before a Court</u>: Persons are entitled to challenge the legal basis or assert the arbitrary nature of their arrest or detention. Judicial inefficiency, corruption, and insufficient resources delayed proceedings, however, and excessively protracted legal processes were a serious problem.

e. Denial of Fair Public Trial

The constitution and law provide for an independent judiciary, but the justice system was poorly funded and staffed, inadequately equipped, often ineffective, and subject to intimidation, corruption, politicization, and patronage. Low salaries and a lack of internal controls rendered judicial officials susceptible to bribery. Powerful special interests, including organized criminal groups, exercised influence on the outcomes of some court proceedings.

In March the president of the Supreme Court disbanded the National Judicial Council, created in 2013 to implement an evaluation system for judges, for corruption and incompetence. The council had allegedly committed contracting irregularities, nepotism, overvalued travel expenses, and other irregular acts. Prosecutors had already charged the vice president of the council with influence peddling for pressuring a judge to drop money-laundering charges against his cousin. He and other members of the council resigned before the president of the Supreme Court formally disbanded the council.

Trial Procedures

The law presumes an accused person is innocent. The accused has the right to an initial hearing before a judge, to ask for bail, to consult with legal counsel in a timely manner, to have a lawyer provided by the state if necessary, and to request an appeal. Defendants can receive free interpretation as necessary from the moment charged through all appeals. The law grants the right to a fair public trial, permits defendants to confront witnesses against them and offer witnesses and evidence in their defense, and grants defendants access to government evidence relevant to their case. Authorities generally respected these rights.

Credible observers noted problems in trial procedures such as a lack of admissible evidence, judicial corruption, widespread public distrust of the legal system, and an ineffective witness protection program (some protected witnesses were killed during the year).

Political Prisoners and Detainees

There were no reports of political prisoners or detainees.

Civil Judicial Procedures and Remedies

The law establishes an independent and impartial judiciary in civil matters, including access to a court to seek damages for human rights violations. Litigants may sue a criminal defendant for damages if authorized by a criminal court. Individuals and organizations may appeal adverse domestic decisions to the Inter-American Human Rights system.

f. Arbitrary or Unlawful Interference with Privacy, Family, Home, or Correspondence

Although the constitution and law generally prohibit such actions, a legal exception allows government authorities to enter a private residence to prevent a crime or in case of other emergency. There were credible complaints that police occasionally failed to obtain the required authorization before entering private homes. As of June the judicial system reported three convictions in 10 alleged cases of illegal entry by government officials.

Ethnic minority rights leaders and farmworker organizations continued to claim that the government failed to redress actions taken by the security forces, government agencies, and private individuals and businesses to dislodge farmers and indigenous people from lands over which they claimed ownership based on land reform laws or ancestral land titles (see section 6, Indigenous People).

Section 2. Respect for Civil Liberties, Including:

a. Freedom of Speech and Press

The constitution and laws provide for freedom of speech and press, with some restrictions, and the government generally respected these rights. A small number of powerful business magnates with intersecting commercial, political, and family ties owned most of the major news media.

Freedom of Speech and Expression: The penal code includes a provision to punish persons who directly, or through public media, incite discrimination, hate, contempt, repression, or violence against a person, group, or organization for reasons of gender, age, sexual orientation, gender identity, political opinion or affiliation, marital status, race or national origin, language, nationality, religion, family affiliation, family or economic situation, disability, health, physical appearance, or any other characteristic that would offend the victim's human dignity.

CONADEH reported that the government closed 21 media outlets that failed to renew their operating licenses, including major opposition channel Globo TV. Some of these channels were already defunct, while others were attempting to renew their broadcast licenses. Many of the affected journalists continued their reporting at other media outlets. Civil society organizations expressed concerns about the allegedly arbitrary nature of the closures.

Violence and Harassment: There were continued reports of harassment and threats against journalists and social communicators (defined as persons not employed as journalists who served as bloggers or conducted public outreach for NGOs). Reports linked most of these instances of harassment and threats to organized criminal elements and gangs.

Government officials at all levels denounced violence and threats of violence against members of the media and social communicators. UNAH's Violence Observatory reported no killings of journalists during the first six months of the year, unlike in the previous year, when nine journalists and social communicators were killed. CONADEH, which used a broader definition than UNAH, reported that 64 journalists, social commentators, and owners and employees of media outlets were killed between 2014 and August. Perpetrators were convicted in three of these cases, and 10 cases were being prosecuted. There were many reports of intimidation and threats against members of the media and their families, including from members of the security forces and from organized crime. It was usually unclear whether violence and threats against journalists were linked to their work or were simply products of generalized violence. For example, reporter Felix Molina was shot and wounded in the second of two apparent attempts to rob him on May 2.

Human rights defenders, including indigenous and environmental rights activists, political activists, labor activists, and representatives of civil society working to combat corruption, reported threats and acts of violence. The killing of Berta Caceres in March (see section 1.a.) was the most emblematic of these cases. Other organizations, including the Indigenous Lenca Movement of La Paz, as well as civil society members of the Special Commission reviewing the HNP, and the leadership of the National Anticorruption Council, reported threats linked to their activities. The AFL-CIO's International Solidarity Center reported threats against several labor leaders, including public-sector labor union leaders (also see section 7.a.).

The Ministry of Human Rights, Justice, Governance, and Decentralization worked to implement the May 2015 Law for the Protection of Human Rights Defenders, Journalists, Social Communicators, and Justice Operators but was hampered by weaknesses in the new protection mechanism, including a lack of staff and other resources. On July 11, the UN Committee on Economic, Social, and Cultural Rights (CESCR) expressed concern that some of the new law's provisions did not assure effective protection for human rights defenders, and that the resources allocated to the protection mechanism were insufficient to ensure the law's effective implementation. NGOs generally criticized the measures as ineffective, based on the small number of persons protected, an overreliance on protective measures provided by police (who many protected persons did not trust), and the limited resources provided to protected persons. Civil society also criticized the government's failure to investigate threats against activists adequately.

The HNP's Human Rights Office continued to implement protective measures for journalists, social communicators, human rights defenders, labor leaders, and other activists receiving threats. On July 19, the government announced it would allocate an additional 10 million lempiras ($434,000) for protection services, essentially doubling the current budget. During the first six months of the year, the government worked with NGO Freedom House to develop and strengthen implementation of the law. As of July 29, the Ministry of Human Rights, Justice, Governance, and Decentralization had received 39 requests for protection since the law's approval in April 2015 and accepted 30, which were being processed. The other nine requests were from persons who were already beneficiaries of IACHR-mandated protection measures that the Human Rights Office of the Ministry of Security continued to implement. The Ministry of Security planned to transfer these cases to the protection mechanism once the government established a formal protocol for doing so. The IACHR had 66 outstanding orders for protection in the country. According to NGO ACI Participa, 49 orders between 2006 and 2015 benefited 426 individuals, including 59 indigenous persons, 27 members of the LGBTI community, 28 environmentalists, and 72 journalists.

The HNP's Violent Crimes Task Force (VCTF) investigated crimes against high-profile and particularly vulnerable victims, including judges, journalists, human rights activists, and members of the LGBTI community. In 2015-16, the VCTF investigated the killings of seven journalists and arrested three suspects in these cases. It also arrested a suspect for the death of a journalist in a prior year, helped bring two other cases to trial, and secured one conviction for the murder of a journalist.

Civil society organizations, including agricultural workers groups and indigenous rights groups, criticized the government and its officials for allegedly criminalizing and stigmatizing social protest. The government charged some members of these groups with trespassing after they occupied disputed land and required them to present themselves to judicial authorities periodically while legal proceedings against them were pending.

Censorship or Content Restrictions: Members of media and NGOs said the press self-censored due to fear of retaliation from organized crime or corrupt government officials.

Libel/Slander Laws: Citizens, including public officials, can initiate criminal proceedings for libel and slander. As of November 3, journalists Julio Ernesto

Alvarado and David Romero Ellner remained free and continued to practice their profession, despite being convicted of slander in 2015 and ordered to stop practicing journalism temporarily. Alvarado paid a fine to avoid jail time; in December 2015 to comply with a 2014 order from the IACHR, the government rescinded the order that he stop practicing journalism. Romero Ellner received a 10-year prison sentence in March, and the Constitutional Chamber of the Supreme Court denied his final appeal on August 19.

National Security: Reporters without Borders and other civil society organizations continued to express concerns about potential abuse of the law for the Classification of Public Documents Related to Defense and National Security. Beginning in the third quarter of 2015, the government made available to the public some information about activities that the security tax and other trust funds support, and it incorporated trust fund numbers into the current budget. In August the Organization of American States' Mission Against Corruption and Impunity in Honduras (MACCIH) and the semiautonomous Institute for Access to Public Information (IAIP) called for the law's revision.

Nongovernmental Impact: Some journalists and other members of civil society reported threats from members of organized crime. It was unclear how many of these threats were related to the victims' professions or activism.

Internet Freedom

The government did not restrict or disrupt access to the internet or censor online content, but there were credible reports that the government monitored private online communications. According to estimates compiled by the International Telecommunication Union, in 2015 approximately 20 percent of the population used the internet.

Academic Freedom and Cultural Events

There were no government restrictions on academic freedom or cultural events.

b. Freedom of Peaceful Assembly and Association.

Freedom of Assembly

The constitution and law provide for freedom of assembly, and the government generally respected this right. Some local and international civil society organizations, including the Civil Council of Popular and Indigenous Organizations of Honduras (COPINH), alleged that members of the security forces used excessive force to break up demonstrations. On several occasions police used tear gas and water cannons to disperse violent protesters. Authorities temporarily detained protesters wielding rocks, machetes, and other dangerous items but usually released them without pressing charges. Many civil society leaders and organizations condemned a decision by UNAH leaders authorizing police to break up a two-month student sit-in in July. Police briefly detained approximately two dozen protest leaders, and university officials then brought criminal charges against them. As of early December, student protesters and UNAH leadership remained in discussions to address the concerns of all parties, including the judicial proceedings and administrative actions that university officials took against protest leaders.

Freedom of Association

The constitution and law provide for freedom of association, and the government generally respected this right. The penal code prohibits illicit association, defined as gatherings by persons bearing arms, explosive devices, or dangerous objects with the purpose of committing a crime, and prescribes prison terms of two to four years and a fine of 30,000 to 60,000 lempiras ($1,300 to $2,600) for anyone who convokes or directs an illicit meeting or demonstration. There were no reports of such cases during the year.

c. Freedom of Religion

See the Department of State's *International Religious Freedom Report* at www.state.gov/religiousfreedomreport/.

d. Freedom of Movement, Internally Displaced Persons, Protection of Refugees, and Stateless Persons

The constitution and law provide for freedom of internal movement, foreign travel, emigration, and repatriation, and the government generally respected these rights. In practical terms there were areas where authorities could not assure freedom of movement because of criminal activity and a lack of significant government presence.

The government cooperated with the Office of the UN High Commissioner for Refugees (UNHCR) and other humanitarian organizations to provide protection and assistance to internally displaced persons, refugees, returning refugees, asylum seekers, stateless persons, and other persons of concern. UNHCR reported that as of August approximately 280 indigenous persons displaced from Nicaragua remained along the international border in Gracias a Dios Department. The government provided some assistance to this community.

Internally Displaced Persons

On April 5, the special rapporteur on the human rights of internally displaced persons welcomed the government's recognition that internal displacement existed in the country and its acknowledgement that the challenges it presents require research and concerted action to tackle its root causes. UNHCR remained concerned about forced displacement caused by high levels of violence, national and transnational gang activity, human trafficking, and migrant smuggling. The government maintained an interinstitutional commission to address the problem of persons displaced by violence. UNHCR reported that it collaborated extensively with the commission, which monitored displacement and developed policies and programs to prevent displacement and to provide protection to displaced persons, focusing on the most vulnerable persons affected by organized crime and other situations of violence. A 2015 UNHCR report estimated there were between 174,000 and 182,000 internally displaced persons in the country. There were no official numbers for forced displacement in the country, in part because gangs controlled many of the neighborhoods that were sources of internal displacement (see section 6, Displaced Children). Media reported in March that gangs ordered residents of two communities, one in San Pedro Sula and one in Tegucigalpa, to vacate their homes; the government responded by increasing law enforcement operations and presence in the affected neighborhoods. Several communities along the border with El Salvador reported that gangs displaced them by moving into their communities, following increased police action in El Salvador. On July 10, authorities lifted a one-month curfew in the town of Mapulaca, in Lempira Department near the border with El Salvador, after increasing security force activities in the area.

Protection of Refugees

The government cooperated with UNHCR and other humanitarian organizations to provide protection and assistance to refugees and other persons of concern.

Access to Asylum: The law allows for the granting of asylum or refugee status. The government has established a system to provide protection to refugees, but at times there were significant delays in processing provisional permits for asylum applicants.

Section 3. Freedom to Participate in the Political Process

The constitution and law provide citizens the right to choose their government in free and fair periodic elections held by secret ballot and based on nearly universal and equal suffrage. The law does not permit active members of the military or the civilian security forces to vote. The constitution prohibits practicing clergy from running for office or participating in political campaigns.

Elections and Political Participation

Recent Elections: In 2013 Juan Orlando Hernandez of the National Party won a four-year presidential term in elections that were generally transparent and credible. Some NGOs reported irregularities, including the distribution of cards offering retail discounts issued near voting stations operated by the National Party, in addition to problems with voter rolls, the buying and selling of electoral workers' credentials, and lack of transparency in campaign financing. International observers acknowledged some of these problems but reported that they were not systematic or widespread enough to affect the outcome of the election. Observers noted several significant improvements in the election's transparency, including electronic scanning and transmission of vote tally sheets and the distribution of national identification cards by the National Registry of Persons rather than by political parties.

In February, Congress elected a new 15-member Supreme Court for a seven-year term. Observers generally recognized the court's election as the most thorough and transparent such process to date.

Participation of Women and Minorities: No laws limit the participation of women and members of minorities in the political process, and women and minorities participated. The law requires a gender balance among each party's candidates running for congress. The National Congress had one representative from the Miskito community. There were no indigenous or Afro-Honduran cabinet members.

Section 4. Corruption and Lack of Transparency in Government

The law provides for criminal penalties on public officials for corruption, but authorities did not implement the law effectively. Government institutions were subject to corruption and political influence, and some officials engaged in corrupt practices with impunity. Insufficient internal controls and lack of training in public resource management contributed to the corruption and lack of transparency. The government took steps to address corruption at high levels in government agencies, including arresting and charging members of congress, judges, prosecutors, current and former senior officials, including presidential staffers from previous administrations, mayors and other local authorities, and police officers.

Following large-scale public protests in the spring of 2015 against government corruption, in January the government signed an agreement with the Organization of American States to install the MACCIH. The MACCIH began operations in the country on April 19, with an initial focus on police reform, electoral reform, and emblematic cases of public sector corruption networks.

Former president Rafael Leonardo Callejas Romero (1990-94) was among 16 persons accused of corruption in 2015 for actions related to the International Federation of Association Football scandal. Callejas surrendered to foreign authorities in December 2015, and on March 28, he pled guilty in a foreign court to eight charges of organized crime, fraud, money laundering, and conspiracy to commit money laundering.

Corruption: Prosecutions of public-sector corruption predominantly targeted low-level officials and focused on charges of abuse of authority and misconduct in public office, which were easier to prove but carried lower penalties than illicit enrichment, fraud, and money laundering. Since the 2014 indictment of the entire board of directors of the Social Security Institute (IHSS), however, there was an increase in indictments of higher-level officials. Since 2014 prosecutors had filed charges against 54 persons in the IHSS scandal, including former ministers, business executives, and labor leaders; prosecutors charged many in multiple cases. As of December 20, there had been five convictions related to the IHSS scandal, including prominent business executive Jose Bertetty. Courts issued three of these convictions during the year. Many cases were in the appeals stage (a case can be appealed before it goes to trial). In June 2015 the government brought charges against public officials at the Ministry of Health and employees of the private company Astropharma, including then vice president of the National Congress, Lena Gutierrez, and three members of her family. In August the court of appeals ruled that the case could continue to trial. On August 8, the Financial Crimes Task Force executed a search warrant at LAIN (International Labs) and seized evidence to support a new line of investigation in the Astropharma case. Trial court judges were selected on September 7. On December 16, former IHSS director Mario Zelaya was convicted on firearms charges; he faced trial on seven additional charges including bribery and money laundering.

There were reports that the government's anticorruption institutions did not take sufficient steps to contain high-level corruption and were unwilling or lacked the professional capacity and resources to investigate, arrest, and prosecute those involved. The civil society organization National Anticorruption Council has an investigative unit of 15 persons. The council receives government funding, which obliges it to disclose the names of its investigators, making them more vulnerable to reprisals. NGOs reported that some individuals who reported public corruption received threats.

In August the domestic NGO (and chapter of Transparency-International), Association for a More Just Society (ASJ) published a report reviewing public corruption in the country for the seven years prior to 2015. The report revealed that during those years the Public Ministry received 3,471 complaints about public corruption and issued 283 indictments. The ASJ tried to review the case files of 165 of the indictments, but it was unable to find 55 case files in the court system. Of the cases it reviewed, nine had resulted in convictions, 29 were resolved without a conviction, and 14 had been open for more than three years without resolution, which the ASJ defined as impunity. In 2015 there were 28 convictions for public-sector corruption, and as of August, there had been 19 such convictions. Among those convicted during the year were two members of Congress, a former government minister, a judge, current and former mayors, and two individuals associated with the IHSS scandal.

Financial Disclosure: Public officials are subject to financial disclosure laws but did not always comply. The law mandates that the Supreme Auditing Tribunal monitor and verify disclosures. The tribunal published its reports on its website and published the names of public officials who did not comply with disclosure laws.

Public Access to Information: The law provides for public access to government information, and the government generally implemented this law effectively. In 2014, however, the National Congress passed a controversial law giving the National Security and Defense Council the authority to classify information that puts national security or defense at risk. NGOs and some members of Congress criticized both the breadth of the law and the manner in which it was approved.

All institutions receiving public funding are required to disclose their expenditures and present an annual report of their activities in the prior year to the National Congress 40 days after the end of the fiscal year. IAIP operated a website through which citizens could request information from government agencies. IAIP is responsible for verifying that government institutions comply with transparency rules and practices for access to public information. In June IAIP reviewed 133 government entities, to include municipalities, on their compliance with transparency regulations. IAIP rated 35 percent of these entities "excellent," 10 percent "good," 12 percent "bad," and 48 percent received its lowest rating of "deficient." IAIP reported that it sanctioned the entities deemed deficient with fines of up to five minimum salaries ($2,000). In July, IAIP also asked the government to suspend 10 officials without pay for five days whose organizations received deficient ratings, including nine mayors, and the Minister of Education, Marlon Escoto, due to his role as rector of the National Agricultural University.

If a government agency denies a request for public information, the denied party can submit a claim to IAIP, which has the authority to fine entities for failing to comply with legitimate requests.

Section 5. Governmental Attitude Regarding International and Nongovernmental Investigation of Alleged Violations of Human Rights

A wide variety of domestic and international human rights groups operated in the country, investigating and publishing their findings on human rights cases. Government officials met with domestic and international NGOs and convened meetings to obtain their views on different issues. Although attentive to NGO views, officials often were not responsive to their recommendations. Some NGOs claimed that some government officials made statements about NGOs that constituted threats or harassment. Citizens may file complaints of human rights violations with the IACHR.

Government Human Rights Bodies: In 2014, as part of a complete restructuring of executive branch agencies, the president combined several ministries to create the Ministry of Human Rights, Justice, Governance, and Decentralization.

As of December the government was implementing 37 recommendations from the 2010 Truth and Reconciliation Commission created after the 2009 political crisis. The recommendations included measures to amend the constitution, increase respect for human rights, and advance efforts to combat corruption.

In 2013 the Council of Ministers approved the government's first Public Policy and National Action Plan for Human Rights, which provides a roadmap for each government ministry to integrate promotion of and respect for human rights into its planning and budget. The administration that took office in 2014 committed to implement the plan. The Ministry of Human Rights, Justice, Governance, and Decentralization reported that as of August, the government had implemented nine of the plan's actions, after implementing 14 actions in 2015. The ministry had provided human rights training to 7,760 persons as of August, including civilian police, members of the armed forces, health- and emergency-service personnel, other government officials, students, businesspersons, and convicts.

The Public Ministry's Office of the Special Prosecutor for Human Rights handled cases involving charges of misconduct by members of the security forces, as well as crimes against communities of special concern. CONADEH performed the functions of an ombudsman and investigated complaints of human rights abuses.

At the invitation of the government, the UN Office of the High Commissioner for Human Rights opened an office in March 2015, but the head of the office did not arrive until October 2016.

Section 6. Discrimination, Societal Abuses, and Trafficking in Persons

Women

<u>Rape and Domestic Violence</u>: Violence against women and impunity for perpetrators continued to be a serious problem. The UNAH Violence Observatory reported 222 violent deaths of women in the first six months of the year, compared with 478 violent deaths of women during 2015.

Rape was a serious and pervasive societal problem. The law criminalizes all forms of rape, including spousal rape. The government considers rape a crime of public concern, and the state prosecutes rapists even if victims do not press charges. Prosecutors treat accusations of spousal rape somewhat differently, however, and evaluate such charges on a case-by-case basis. The penalties for rape range from three to nine years' imprisonment, and the courts enforced these penalties. Rape continued to be underreported, however, due to fear of stigma, retribution, and further violence. The Center for Women's Rights (CDM) reported that 2,774 women and girls reported sexual crimes to the Public Ministry in 2015. As of October the Public Ministry's Office of Crimes Against Women had received

1,172 formal complaints of domestic violence and provided 2,989 legal consultations. The CDM also reported that the Public Ministry's General Directorate for Forensic Medicine conducted 3,022 examinations of sexual violence survivors in 2015, a 40 percent increase over 2014. According to reports from victims, 73 percent of attackers were family members or other individuals the victims knew.

Violence between domestic and intimate partners continued to be widespread. The law provides penalties of up to four years in prison for domestic violence; however, if a victim's physical injuries do not reach the severity required to categorize the violence as a criminal act, the only legal penalty for a first offense is a sentence of one to three months of community service. Female victims of domestic violence are entitled to certain protective measures. Abusers caught in the act may be detained for up to 24 hours as a preventive measure. The law provides a maximum sentence of three years in prison for disobeying a restraining order connected with the crime of intra-familial violence. In many cases victims were reluctant to press charges against their abusers because of economic dependence on their male partners, their roles in caring for children, and a lack of domestic violence shelters. The CDM reported that 18,070 women filed complaints of domestic violence in special domestic violence courts in 2015.

The government provided services to victims of domestic violence in hospitals and health centers. The national government provided space through September for an NGO in Tegucigalpa to run a shelter, and provided police protection. Local governments, in cooperation with NGOs, operated domestic violence shelters in San Pedro Sula, Choluteca, La Ceiba, and Juticalpa; they also had an office in Comayagua. NGOs operated their own small shelters in Santa Rosa de Copan and Comayagua. The government did not provide enough financial and other resources for these facilities to operate effectively.

In cooperation with the UN Development Program, the government operated consolidated reporting centers in Tegucigalpa and San Pedro Sula where women could report crimes, seek medical and psychological attention, and receive other services. These reporting centers were in addition to the 298 government-operated women's offices--one in each municipality--that provided a wide array of services to women, focusing on education, personal finance, health, social and political participation, environmental stewardship, and prevention of gender-based violence. The quantity and quality of services that these offices provided was uneven. CONADEH reported that in 2015, 37 percent of the 3,372 complaints it received for violations of women's rights were for domestic violence, 22 percent were for lack of access to justice and due process, and 41 percent were for alleged violations of economic, social, and cultural rights.

In March 2015 the UN special rapporteur on violence against women expressed concern that most women in the country remained marginalized, discriminated against, and at high risk of being subjected to human rights violations, including violence and violations of their sexual and reproductive rights. UN Women reported in 2015 that violent deaths of women and girls, domestic violence, and sexual violence in all forms increased steadily from 2005 to 2014, but UNAH's Violence Observatory reported a drop in violent deaths of women between 2013 (636 deaths) and the first six months of the year (222 deaths).

Sexual Harassment: Both the penal and labor codes criminalize various forms of sexual harassment. Violators face penalties of one to three years in prison and possible suspension of their professional licenses, but the government did not effectively enforce the law. Sexual harassment was a serious societal problem but was underreported because of fear of stigma and reprisal. The CDM reported that 94 women filed complaints of sexual harassment in the workplace in 2015. The Supreme Court reported receiving only two cases of sexual harassment in 2015 and none in the first six months of the year. In that time one case was brought to trial, four cases were dismissed, two provisionally dismissed, and one case resolved through mediation.

Reproductive Rights: Generally, couples and individuals have the right to decide freely the number, spacing, and timing of their children; manage their reproductive health; and have access to the information and means to do so, free from discrimination, coercion, or violence. According to UN estimates, maternal mortality was approximately 129 deaths per 100,000 live births in 2015, and the lifetime risk of maternal death was 1 in 300. Although 83 percent of births were attended by skilled health personnel, the UN Population Fund (UNFPA) reported that there were significant gaps in emergency obstetric care.

The Ministry of Health also worked to expand the provision of family planning services in rural and low-income areas. UNFPA estimated in 2015 that 64 percent of women between the ages of 15 and 49 used a modern contraceptive method, and 11 percent of women had an unmet family planning need. Family planning supplies continued to be limited by shortages and insufficient funding.

There were reports of forced sterilizations of women with HIV, according to the International AIDS Society.

NGOs criticized a 2009 prohibition on emergency contraception medication, which they claimed abridged a woman's right to make family planning decisions. According to the Guttmacher Institute, selling, distributing, or using emergency contraception carried the same punishments as performing or obtaining abortion, for which the Center for Reproductive Rights reported that women can be sentenced to three to six years in prison; no cases of enforcement were known to be reported.

Discrimination: Although the law accords women and men the same legal rights and status, including property rights in divorce cases, many women did not fully enjoy such rights. On July 11, the CESCR expressed concern that women living in rural areas, indigenous women, and women of African descent continued to be victims of multiple and cross-sectoral forms of discrimination, as reflected in their high rates of poverty. Most women in the workforce engaged in lower-status and lower-paying informal occupations, such as domestic service, without the benefit of legal protections. Women participated in small numbers in most professions, but cultural attitudes limited their career opportunities. Women participated in the formal labor force at approximately one-half the rate of men. By law women have equal access to educational opportunities. The law requires that employers pay women equal wages for equal work, but often classified women's jobs as less demanding than those of men to justify women's lower salaries. Job seekers older than age 30, particularly women, faced age discrimination.

Children

Birth Registration: Children derive citizenship by birth in the country, from the citizenship of their parents, or by naturalization. Although birth registration was widely available in 2015, the UN Children's Fund (UNICEF) reported that, according to the National Population and Housing Census of 2013, an estimated 65,000 children did not have birth registration documents. The largest numbers of unregistered children were in indigenous and Afro-Honduran communities. UNICEF assisted the government in extending civil registries to indigenous and remote communities, and, as of 2015, the government had 217 automated registration offices. Only seven registration offices lacked automation, all of them located in isolated areas that lacked electricity.

Education: Education is free, compulsory, and universal through the 12th grade, although high school students had to pay fees. There was a shortage of middle schools and adequately prepared teachers. According to 2013 census data, girls generally attended at a higher rate than boys did, a gap that widened after age 12. By age 15 there were 6 percent fewer boys in school than girls.

Child Abuse: Child abuse remained a serious problem. The UNAH Violence Observatory reported 412 cases of mistreatment and abandonment of children in 2015. The law establishes prison sentences of up to three years for child abuse.

The Violence Observatory reported the homicides of 570 children--88 girls and 482 boys--in 2015, a 9 percent decrease from 2014. NGOs stated that these figures probably underestimated the number of crimes against children. As of July the children's rights organization, Casa Alianza, reported the homicides and violent deaths of 147 children; there were no arrests in 80 percent of these cases. The Violence Observatory reported 117 such homicides, a more than 50 percent decrease from 2015. Casa Alianza said the homicides often involved torture, strangulation, and dumping bodies in remote areas. While there were some improvements in the overall security situation, there were reports that police committed acts of violence against poor youths. Human rights groups continued to allege that private citizens and individual members of the security forces used unwarranted lethal force against youths.

Because the country's antigang legislation specifies lower penalties for minors, gangs continued to employ underage youth in their operations. Children from eight to 12 years old frequently worked as lookouts and collected "war taxes" (that is, extortion payments). Consequently, rival gangs often disputed recruiting areas around schools.

Five street children between the ages of 13 and 16, who were working without authorization to collect and recycle garbage, were killed on February 11 in Tegucigalpa. Media reported that gang members were presumed responsible for the deaths.

Early and Forced Marriage: The minimum legal age for marriage is 21, although with parental consent boys may marry at 18 and girls at 16. According to government statistics, 10 percent of women marry before age 15 and 37 percent before age 18.

Sexual Exploitation of Children: The commercial sexual exploitation of children, especially in prostitution, continued to be a problem. The country was a destination for child sex tourism. The legal age of consent is 18. There is no statutory rape law, but the penalty for rape of a minor under age 12 is 15 to 20 years in prison. The penalty is nine to 13 years in prison if the victim is age 13 or older. Penalties for facilitating child prostitution are 10 to 15 years in prison, with fines ranging from one million to 2.5 million lempiras ($44,000 to $110,000). The law prohibits the use of children under 18 for exhibitions or performances of a sexual nature or in the production of pornography.

Displaced Children: Many children lived on the streets. Casa Alianza estimated there were more than 8,800 street children in major cities. Between September 2015 and August, Casa Alianza assisted 256 street children, 38 more than in the previous 12 months. During the same period, the organization assisted 400 children in its shelters and helped 75 children reintegrate with their families.

Polling indicated that lack of economic and educational opportunities, fear of violence, and the desire for family reunification motivated children to seek to emigrate. One civil society organization reported that common causes of forced displacement for youth included death threats for failure to pay extortion, attempted recruitment by gangs, witnessing criminal activity by gangs or organized crime, domestic violence, attempted kidnappings, family members' involvement in drug dealing, victimization by traffickers, discrimination based on sexual orientation, sexual harassment, and discrimination for having a chronic illness. Casa Alianza reported that as of July 4, the Belen migrant attention center in San Pedro Sula had processed 417 youths deported from Mexico. Casa Alianza identified 261 of these youths as persons displaced by violence.

Institutionalized Children: Between January 2015 and September 2016, at least 10 juveniles were killed while in detention in government facilities, nine of them in the Renaciendo center. CONAPREV reported four incidents at Renaciendo as of August, including violence between members of MS-18 and another gang, Los Chirizos, resulting in the deaths of two minors affiliated with Los Chirizos and injuries to 11 other detainees.

International Child Abductions: The country is a party to the 1980 Hague Convention on the Civil Aspects of International Child Abduction. See the Department of State's *Annual Report on International Parental Child Abduction* at travel.state.gov/content/childabduction/en/legal/compliance.html.

Anti-Semitism

The Jewish community, located primarily in San Pedro Sula, numbered several hundred. There were no known reports of anti-Semitic acts.

Trafficking in Persons

See the Department of State's *Trafficking in Persons Report* at
www.state.gov/j/tip/rls/tiprpt/.

Persons with Disabilities

The law prohibits discrimination against persons with physical, sensory,
intellectual, and mental disabilities in employment, education, air travel and other
transportation, access to health care, access to the judicial system, or the provision
of other state services. Enforcement in the area of employment is the
responsibility of the Secretariat of State for Labor and Social Security (STSS), but
was not effective due to the STSS's limited resources and its focus on workplace
safety and pay. The Public Ministry is responsible for prosecuting violations. The
law requires that persons with disabilities have access to buildings, but few
buildings were accessible, and the national government did not effectively
implement laws or programs to provide such access.

The law includes provisions for inclusive education of students with disabilities.
In June the Ministry of Education reported that there were 63,148 students with
disabilities in the school system. Also in June the National Federation of Parents
of Individuals with Disabilities in Honduras signed an agreement with the ministry
to work together to monitor and evaluate the ministry's Institutional Management
Plan for Universal Access to Educational Facilities. The ministry agreed to devote
one-third of new teaching positions to facilities that have children with disabilities.
In July the ministry announced that more than 6,000 educational centers had
conducted analyses of access for children with disabilities and that it would use
these analyses to assign necessary staff in 2017. An additional 1,725 educational
centers in seven departments had conducted accessibility studies and created
accessibility plans. On August 26, the ministry announced it had filled 349 staff
positions, including more than 200 new technical assistant positions, in schools
having children with disabilities and in indigenous communities. Some parents
filed complaints against schools that allegedly refused to register students with
disabilities. In 2014 CONADEH estimated that 27 percent of economically active
individuals with disabilities had no education and 56 percent had only a primary
education.

The government continued to struggle to implement its policy on persons with disabilities. The government had a disabilities unit in the Ministry of Development and Social Inclusion.

National /Racial/Ethnic Minorities

In the 2013 census, approximately 8.5 percent of the population identified themselves as members of indigenous communities, but other estimates were higher. Indigenous groups including the Miskito, Tawahkas, Pech, Tolupans, Lencas, Maya-Chortis, Nahual, Bay Islanders, and Garifunas had limited representation in the national government and consequently little direct input into decisions affecting their lands, cultures, traditions, and the allocation of natural resources.

According to government data, 89 percent of indigenous and Afro-descendent children lived in poverty, 78 percent of them in extreme poverty. In 2014 the UN Committee on the Elimination of Racial Discrimination expressed concerns about persistent poverty among indigenous peoples and Afro-descendent communities, as well as their social exclusion. It noted in particular that women in Afro-Honduran and indigenous communities faced multiple forms of discrimination in all aspects of social, political, and economic life. On April 11, the government adopted a Policy against Racism and Racial Discrimination for the Comprehensive Development of the Indigenous and African-Honduran Populations.

The 2013 census reported that 15 percent of male and 17.5 percent of female indigenous persons 10 years and older had no education. The National Institute of Statistics estimated in 2015 that 21 percent of the general population was illiterate, with an illiteracy rate of 36 percent among those ages 60 and over. Illiteracy rates were more than double that in rural areas. Sixty percent of indigenous respondents above the age of 10 reported having a sixth-grade education or less. The Directorate General for Intercultural Multilingual Education began operating in 2013 with a mission to expand educational opportunities in both Spanish and local languages. In 2015 the Ministry of Education increased by 48,000, to 119,000, the number of students educated in bilingual schools that teach in both Spanish and a local language.

Indigenous People

On July 21, the UN special rapporteur on the rights of indigenous peoples categorized the situation of the indigenous peoples of the country as critical. She stated that their rights over their lands, territories, and natural resources were not protected, that they faced acts of violence when claiming their rights in a general environment of violence and impunity, and that they lacked access to justice. Additionally, they suffered from inequality, poverty, and a lack of basic social services such as education and healthcare.

On March 3, indigenous and environmental rights activist Berta Caceres was killed in her home. At the time of her death, Caceres was leading opposition to the Agua Zarca hydroelectric project in Intibuca Department. She was granted protective measures from the IACHR and some protective services from the government. In May the government arrested four individuals for involvement in her death. Subsequently, authorities arrested two additional suspects. As of December 20, all six remained in custody pending trial following initial evidentiary hearings. As of December human rights groups, indigenous groups, and members of the Caceres family continued to press authorities to identify and arrest those that ordered her murder, whom they suspected were still at large.

Two of those arrested had links to Desarrollos Energeticos, SA (DESA), the company constructing the dam. Some local community members, including Caceres, opposed the project and claimed that the government had failed to consult appropriately with the indigenous Lenca community as required under International Labor Organization (ILO) Convention 169; they also criticized DESA for failing to consult with the indigenous community. Other community members, however, supported the project as a source of local employment and development. Although the country has no law defining how to implement ILO 169, in August the Public Ministry began criminal proceedings against the former vice minister of the environment who awarded the concession for the project and against the mayor of the town where it was set to be built. The Public Ministry accused them of abuse of authority and failure to abide by the international obligations of ILO 169. In November a judge ordered another former vice minister of the environment held without bail pending trial for abuse of authority and failure to abide by the international obligations of ILO 169 when authorizing changes to the Agua Zarca hydroelectric project.

Other indigenous and environmental rights activists also reported threats and acts of violence against them. Ana Mirian Romero of the Indigenous Lenca Movement of La Paz reported receiving death threats and said someone burned her house down. Caceres' organization, COPINH, reported threats and violence against other members as well. The government took some steps to investigate and arrest those responsible for the violence.

As of September the government was in discussions with indigenous communities over a bill that would regulate prior consultation under ILO 169. As of early November, COPINH and Garifuna indigenous organization OFRANEH decided not to participate in the discussions and instead supported a separate bill presented in Congress earlier in the year. On July 11, CESCR expressed concerns about reports that the government had failed to respect indigenous peoples' right to prior consultation. CESCR insisted that such consultations were necessary to obtain these communities' input on decisions that could affect them, including when negotiating concessions for the exploitation of natural resources or other development projects.

Communal ownership was the norm for most indigenous land, providing land-use rights for individual members of the community. Documents dating to the mid-19th century defined indigenous land titles poorly. The government continued its efforts to recognize indigenous titles. Lack of clear land titles provoked land use conflicts with nonindigenous agricultural laborers, businesses, and government entities interested in developing coastlines, forests, areas rich in mineral resources, and other lands that indigenous and other ethnic minority communities traditionally occupied or used. Indigenous communities criticized the government's alleged complicity in the exploitation of timber and other natural resources on these lands. Indigenous leaders continued to allege that indigenous and nonindigenous groups smuggled drugs and other contraband through their lands and illegally appropriated vast areas of their communal lands.

In October 2015 the Inter-American Court of Human Rights ruled in favor of two Garifuna communities that had accused the government of violating their rights by failing to protect their communities' land from exploitation. As of December, the government was working to create a mechanism to address the ramifications of these rulings.

The government formally recognized nine indigenous and Afro-descendent communities and continued efforts to address indigenous land rights problems. In April the government completed the transfer of land titles to the 12 Miskito territorial councils, including two titles to land in the Rio Platano biosphere. Since 2012 the territorial councils received titles to more than 5,400 square miles, 12 percent of the country's territory. NGOs helped indigenous communities negotiate with the government and establish their juridical identities.

Persons from indigenous and Afro-descendent communities continued to experience discrimination in employment, education, housing, and health services.

Acts of Violence, Discrimination, and Other Abuses Based on Sexual Orientation and Gender Identity

The law states that sexual orientation and gender identity characteristics merit special protection from discrimination and includes these characteristics in a hate crimes amendment to the penal code. Nevertheless, social discrimination against LGBTI persons was widespread. As of October the special prosecutor for human rights was investigating nine formal complaints of discrimination by members of the LGBTI community in previous years. Representatives of NGOs that focused on the right to sexual diversity alleged that the PMOP and other elements of the security forces harassed and abused members of the community. As of August the NGO Colectivo Color Rosa reported 11 violent deaths of LGBTI persons, similar to levels in previous years. In October the Public Ministry reported records of 218 cases of violent deaths of LGBTI individuals since 2009, of which 14 cases had resulted in convictions and 171 were still under investigation. NGOs also documented multiple instances of assaults and discrimination against members of the LGBTI community.

On June 2, prominent LGBTI activist and community leader Rene Martinez was killed. Martinez was an activist in the ruling National Party, the president of an LGBTI association in San Pedro Sula, the leader of a local community council, and a volunteer with a community-based violence prevention program. As of early August, the VCTF continued to investigate the case. It was uncertain whether his death was related to his LGBTI status or political activities.

LGBTI rights groups asserted that government agencies and private employers engaged in discriminatory hiring practices. LGBTI groups continued working with the VCTF, the Ministry of Security, and the Office of the Special Prosecutor for Human Rights to address concerns about intimidation, fear of reprisals, and police corruption.

In April the HNP assigned 30 new agents to the VCTF, bringing the total to 41 VCTF investigators. As of September the new investigators were going through a training and mentorship phase, after which the HNP would assign them either in Tegucigalpa or San Pedro Sula. As of September the VCTF was investigating 17 homicides of members of the LGBTI community. The VCTF arrested two suspects from cases initiated during the year and one suspect from a case initiated in 2015.

The HNP took steps to educate personnel to respond more effectively to cases of gender-based violence and violence against LGBTI persons. The Criminal Investigations School (EIC) designed two new police education modules, one on gender-based violence awareness and the other on LGBTI violence reduction. These modules were included in all EIC courses for recruits beginning on August 22.

HIV and AIDS Social Stigma

Access to employment, educational opportunities, and health services continued to be major challenges for persons with HIV/AIDS. One civil society organization reported that three members of the LGBTI community died of gunshot wounds after medical personnel refused to treat them because they would not submit to HIV tests. Community members reported that transgender women were particularly vulnerable to discrimination, and that many could find employment only as sex workers.

Section 7. Worker Rights

a. Freedom of Association and the Right to Collective Bargaining

The law grants workers the right to form and join unions of their choice, bargain collectively, and strike. It prohibits employer retribution against employees for engaging in trade union activities. The law places a number of restrictions on these rights, such as requiring that a recognized trade union represent at least 30 workers, prohibiting foreign nationals from holding union offices, and requiring that union officials work in the same substantive area of the business as the workers they represent. Following an employer's appeal of the findings of a 2015 labor inspection, in October the STSS administratively ruled that seasonal workers could not hold leadership positions in a union. Labor unions filed an appeal of this decision in October, saying it violated labor rights and international standards. The law prohibits members of the armed forces and police, as well as certain other public employees, from forming labor unions.

The law requires an employer to begin collective bargaining once workers establish a union, and specifies that if more than one union exists at a company the employer must negotiate with the largest.

The law allows only local unions to call strikes, prohibits labor federations and confederations from calling strikes, and requires that a two-thirds majority of both union and nonunion employees at an enterprise approve a strike. The law prohibits workers from legally striking until after they have attempted and failed to come to agreement with their employer, and it requires workers and employers to participate in a mediation and conciliation process. Additionally, the law prohibits strikes in a wide range of economic activities that the government has designated as essential services or that it considers would affect the rights of individuals in the larger community to security, health, education, and economic and social well-being.

The law prohibits certain public service employees from striking. The law permits workers in public health care, social security, staple food production, and public utilities (municipal sanitation, water, electricity, and telecommunications) to strike, as long as they continue to provide basic services. The law also requires that public-sector workers involved in the refining, transportation, and distribution of petroleum products submit their grievances to the STSS before striking. The ILO expressed concerns that restricting strikes in so many sectors was excessive. The law permits strikes by workers in export processing zones and free zones for companies that provide services to industrial parks, but it requires that strikes not impede the operations of other factories in such parks.

The STSS has the power to declare a work stoppage illegal, and employers may discipline employees consistent with their internal regulations, including firing strikers, if the STSS rules that a strike is illegal. The ILO expressed concerns about the government's authority to end disputes in several sectors, including oil production and transport, because such authority is vulnerable to abuse.

The government did not effectively enforce the law. The STSS can fine companies that violate the right to freedom of association. The law permits fines of between 200 and 10,000 lempiras ($9 to $440) per violation. If a company unlawfully dismisses founding union members or union leaders, the law stipulates that employers must also pay a fine equivalent to six months of the dismissed leaders' salaries to the union itself. Civil society, international organizations, and the STSS complained that such small fines failed to deter violations. In practice the STSS rarely imposed or collected fines for violations. When the STSS imposed fines, inspectors had to clear them through the Central Office of the Inspector General, a requirement that added a year or more to the time between an inspection and a fine. Both the STSS and the courts may order a company to reinstate workers, but the

STSS lacks the means to ensure compliance. The reinstatement process in the courts was unduly long, lasting from six months to more than five years.

Workers had difficulty exercising the rights to form and join unions and to engage in collective bargaining, and the government failed to enforce applicable laws effectively. Public-sector trade unionists raised concerns about government interference in trade union activities, including its suspension or ignoring of collective agreements and its dismissals of union members and leaders.

Due to suspicions that employees at the STSS's registry office alerted companies when workers were attempting to unionize--thereby facilitating the dismissal of union organizers before they gained additional legal protections--some unions delayed providing lists of members to the STSS until after the union formally notified the employer of its formation. Although there is no legal requirement that they do so, STSS inspectors generally accompanied workers when they notified their employer of their intent to form a union. In some cases STSS inspectors, rather than workers, directly notified employers of workers' intent to organize. Workers reported that the presence and participation of the STSS reduced the risk that employers would dismiss the union's founders and later claim they were unaware of efforts to unionize.

Civil servants frequently engaged in illegal work stoppages without experiencing reprisals, but there were also reports that government employees, including sanitation workers and police officers, lost their jobs or were subjected to discipline for striking over working conditions. Medical professionals and others continued to hold strikes throughout the year to protest arrears in salary and overtime.

Some employers either refused to engage in collective bargaining or made it very difficult to do so. Some companies also delayed appointing or failed to appoint representatives for required STSS-led mediation, a practice that prolonged the mediation process and impeded the right to strike. There were allegations that companies used collective pacts, which are collective contracts with nonunionized workers, to prevent unionization and collective bargaining because only one collective contract can exist in each workplace. Unions also raised concerns about the use of temporary contracts and part-time employment, suggesting that employers used these mechanisms to prevent unionization and avoid providing full benefits. A Supreme Court ruling requires that both unions and employers notify the STSS of new collective agreements before they go into effect. There were some complaints that employers delayed making such notifications.

Antiunion discrimination continued to be a serious problem. The three major union federations and several civil society groups noted that many companies paid the fines that government authorities imposed but continued to violate the law. Some failed to remedy violations despite multiple visits by STSS inspectors. Employers often threatened to close unionized factories and harassed or dismissed workers seeking to unionize. Local unions, the AFL-CIO's International Solidarity Center, and other organizations reported that some employers dismissed union leaders in attempts to undermine union operations. As of August the Solidarity Center reported that it was aware of 25 cases of individuals fired for union activism. In 2015 the STSS levied 650,000 lempiras ($28,500) in fines against 134 companies for labor rights violations. As part of a bilateral Monitoring and Action Plan signed by the minister of labor in December 2015, the government agreed to increase fines for violations of labor laws through a new labor inspection law. The International Solidarity Center reported threats against several labor leaders, including public-sector labor union leaders.

Employers often further complicated matters by barring STSS inspectors from entering company premises to serve union protection documents. STSS inspectors rarely called on police to help them gain entry to a factory. Employers often failed to comply with STSS orders requiring them to reinstate workers fired for engaging in union activities. As of September NGOs documented eight cases of threats or violence against union leaders during the year, including leaders in the agricultural and public sectors.

There was credible evidence that some employers in the manufacturing industry continued to blacklist employees who sought to form unions. Some companies in other sectors, including the banana industry, established employer-controlled unions that prevented the formation of independent unions because of legal restrictions on the number of unions and collective bargaining agreements allowed per company.

Several companies in export processing zones had solidarity associations that functioned similarly to company unions for the purposes of setting wages and negotiating working conditions.

b. Prohibition of Forced or Compulsory Labor

The law prohibits all forms of forced labor, but the government did not effectively implement or enforce these laws. Administrative penalties of up to 5,000 lempiras

($220) were insufficient to deter violations and were rarely enforced. Penalties for forced labor under antitrafficking laws range from 10 to 15 years' imprisonment, but authorities often did not enforce them. As of August the government was investigating two cases of labor trafficking, one of street children forced to work as beggars and another involving domestic service.

Forced labor occurred in street vending, domestic service, the transport of drugs and other illicit goods, and other criminal activity. Victims were primarily impoverished men, women, and children in both rural and urban areas (also see section 7.c.). The 2015 prison labor law requiring prisoners to work at least five hours a day, six days a week, took effect in January. Regulations for implementing the law were still under development as of December 20. The Ministry of Human Rights, Justice, Governance, and Decentralization said it was taking every precaution to protect prisoners' rights and assure that the work provided opportunities for prisoners to develop skills they could use in legal economic activities after their release.

Also see the Department of State's *Trafficking in Persons Report* at www.state.gov/j/tip/rls/tiprpt/.

c. Prohibition of Child Labor and Minimum Age for Employment

The law regulates child labor, sets the minimum age for employment at 14, and regulates the hours and types of work that minors up to age 18 may perform. By law all minors between 14 and 18 years old must receive special permission from the STSS to work, and the STSS must perform a home study to verify that there is an economic need for the child to work and that the child will not work outside the country or in hazardous conditions, including in offshore fishing. The STSS approved 132 such authorizations between 2014 and August. The vast majority of children who worked did so without STSS permits. If the STSS grants permission, children between 14 and 16 years old may work a maximum of four hours a day, and those between 16 and 18 years old may work up to six hours a day. The law prohibits night work and overtime for minors under the age of 18, but the STSS can grant special permission for minors ages 16 to 18 to work in the evening if such employment does not adversely affect their education.

The law requires that individuals and companies that employ more than 20 school-age children at their facilities provide a location for a school.

The government did not devote adequate resources or sufficient inspectors to monitor compliance with child labor laws or to prevent or pursue violations. Fines for child labor are between 5,000 lempiras ($220) and 25,000 lempiras ($1,100) for a first violation, and as high as 50,000 lempiras ($2,200) for repeat violations. These fines are higher than those for other violations of the labor code. The law also imposes prison sentences of three to five years for child labor violations that endanger the life or morality of a child. The STSS did not effectively enforce child labor laws, except in the apparel assembly sector, and there were frequent violations. The STSS issued 35 fines in 2015 for child labor violations. As of September the STSS had identified 14 small businesses that employed children, and fined seven of them.

Estimates of the number of children under age 18 in the country's workforce range from 370,000 to 510,000. During the year the Ministry of Education reported that 32,719 students in grades one through 12 were working. Children often worked on coffee, okra, and sugarcane plantations; rummaged at garbage dumps; worked in the forestry, hunting, and fishing sectors; worked as domestic servants; peddled goods such as fruit; begged; washed cars; hauled goods; and labored in limestone quarrying and lime production. Most child labor occurred in rural areas. Children often worked alongside family members in agriculture and other work, such as fishing, construction, transportation, and small businesses. Some of the worst forms of child labor occurred, including commercial sexual exploitation of children, and NGOs reported that gangs often forced children to commit crimes, including murder (see section 6, Children).

Also see the Department of Labor's *Findings on the Worst Forms of Child Labor* at www.dol.gov/ilab/reports/child-labor/findings/.

d. Discrimination with Respect to Employment and Occupation

The law prohibits discrimination based on gender, age, sexual orientation, gender identity, political opinion or affiliation, marital status, race or national origin, language, nationality, religion, family affiliation, family or economic situation, disability, health, physical appearance, or any other characteristic that would offend the victim's human dignity. Penalties include prison sentences of up to five years and monetary fines. The law prohibits employers from requiring pregnancy tests as a prerequisite for employment; violators are subject to a 5,000 lempira ($220) fine. The government did not effectively enforce these laws and regulations.

Many employers discriminated against women. According to a 2013 study by the National Institute for Women, employers paid women an average of 16 percent less than they paid men for comparable work. Female workers in the textile export industry continued to report being required to take pregnancy tests as a condition of employment. Persons with disabilities, indigenous and Afro-Honduran persons, LGBTI persons, and persons with HIV/AIDS also faced discrimination in employment and occupation (also see section 6, Children). As of August the STSS reported that it had received no formal complaints of work discrimination. The International Solidarity Center reported that the STSS had received 12 complaints of discrimination based on disability.

e. Acceptable Conditions of Work

There are 42 categories of monthly minimum wages, based on the industry and the size of a company's workforce; the minimums range from 5,682 lempiras ($250) to 9,593 lempiras ($420). The law does not cover domestic workers.

The law applies equally to citizens and foreigners, regardless of gender, and prescribes a maximum eight-hour shift per day for most workers, a 44-hour workweek, and at least one 24-hour rest period for every six days of work. It also provides for paid national holidays and annual leave. The law requires overtime pay, bans excessive compulsory overtime, limits overtime to four hours a day for a maximum workday of 12 hours, and prohibits the practice of requiring workers to complete work quotas before leaving their place of employment. The law does not protect domestic workers effectively.

In 2015 the government approved a new social security law. As part of the new law, employers must deposit at least 50 percent of the severance pay to which an employee is entitled into a bank account in the employee's name. This provision, however, remained suspended as of December 20, pending the resolution of several court cases and further clarification of how the law will be implemented.

Occupational safety and health standards were current but not enforced. By law workers may remove themselves from situations that endanger their health or safety without jeopardizing continued employment.

The STSS is responsible for enforcing the national minimum wage, hours of work, and occupational health and safety laws, but it did so inconsistently and ineffectively. The law permits fines of up to 1,000 lempiras ($45) for failing to pay the minimum wage, 500 lempiras ($22) for violating occupational safety or health regulations, and 5,000 lempiras ($220) for other labor code violations. As part of the Monitoring and Action Plan, the government nearly doubled the budget for inspectors, from 31.127 million lempiras ($1.4 million) to 59.54 million lempiras ($2.6 million). As of August inspectors had conducted 11,494 inspections, including 3,163 at work sites and 8,331 at STSS offices. As of August the STSS had 136 labor inspectors.

Because labor inspectors continued to be concentrated in Tegucigalpa and San Pedro Sula, full labor inspections and follow-up visits to confirm compliance were far less frequent in other parts of the country. Many inspectors asked workers to provide them with transportation so that they could conduct inspections, since the STSS did not have sufficient resources to pay for travel to worksites. Credible allegations of corruption among labor inspectors continued. Inspectors repeatedly failed to respond to requests for inspections to address alleged violations of labor laws, did not impose or collect fines when they discovered violations, and did not ensure enforcement of remediation orders.

Authorities did not effectively enforce worker safety standards, particularly in the construction, garment assembly, and agricultural sectors, as well as in the informal economy. The STSS conducted 31 reinspections of companies identified as labor rights violators under a Dominican Republic-Central America Free Trade Agreement (CAFTA-DR) complaint filed in 2012 by labor unions. Employers rarely paid the minimum wage in the agricultural sector and paid it inconsistently in other sectors. Employers frequently penalized agricultural workers for taking legally established days off.

There were reports of violations of overtime limits, with agricultural workers allegedly working seven days a week for many months. There were credible allegations of compulsory overtime at apparel assembly factories--particularly for women, who made up approximately 65 percent of the sector's workforce--as well as in the private security sector and among domestic workers. Employers frequently denied workers mandatory benefits, including vacation pay and 13th- and 14th-month bonuses. As of August the STSS had recovered 26.91 million lempiras ($1.2 million) in unpaid severance from four companies and was working with an additional three companies to complete collection of outstanding severance payments from them. There were reports that both public- and private-sector employers failed to pay into the social security system.

Human rights organizations continued to report that workers in the private security and domestic sectors were typically obliged to work more than 60 hours a week, but were paid for only 44. Domestic workers often lacked contracts and received salaries below a living wage. Since many lived in on-site quarters, their work hours varied widely based on the will of individual employers. Private security guards also often worked for salaries below the minimum wage. Many guards worked every two days on 24-hour shifts, in violation of the law. Civil society organizations also reported that employers often forced workers in cleaning services and the fast food industry to work shifts of 12 hours or more. The STSS regularly received complaints of failure to pay agreed overtime, especially in the security and cleaning service sectors. As of August the STSS had received 85 formal complaints of failure to pay overtime and fined 57 companies for not doing so. The STSS estimated that more than 60 percent of workers were employed in the informal economy.

There continued to be reports of violations of occupational health and safety laws affecting the approximately 3,000 persons who made a living by diving for seafood such as lobster, conch, and sea cucumber, most from the Miskito indigenous community and other ethnic minority groups in Gracias a Dios Department. These violations included lack of access to appropriate safety equipment. In 2014 the UN Committee on the Elimination of Racial Discrimination raised similar concerns, calling the working conditions "deplorable." Civil society groups reported that most dive boats held more than twice the craft's capacity for divers and that many boat captains sold their divers marijuana and crack cocaine to help them complete an average of 12 dives a day, to depths of more than 100 feet. In 2014 the government banned compressed air diving for sea cucumbers because of deaths in the dive fisheries. The STSS inspected 45 fishing boats at the opening of the season. As of September 20, the Honduran Miskito Association of Crippled Divers (AMHBLI) reported five deaths and 15 injuries. AMHBLI reported the deaths of 455 divers and the crippling of 1,750 others since 1988.